ANI AFSHAR

BEADED FANTASIES
Beads & Wires Jewelry

A Step-by-Step Workshop

Photography by
Jeffrey B. Snyder

Schiffer® Publishing Ltd
4880 Lower Valley Road Atglen, Pennsylvania 19310

Foreword

Integrity is the word that comes to mind when I think of the work of ANI AFSHAR. I've met and worked with many, many artists, and designers over the years – rarely have I come across someone with such clear and focused design intention.

Using bead, wire, fiber, and ribbon, Ani creates a very special vocabulary of texture and volume. The reductive silhouettes that she creates often belie the intricate and precise nature of her technique. As a designer myself, I am in awe of the hand agility required in this medium. Ani is the master.

The craft of weaving and bead manipulation is an ancient one. Ani employs this sense of history and, at the same time, succeeds in creating a very contemporary sensibility. Make no mistake - Ani Afshar is a modernist.

I feel honored to have ANI AFSHAR'S work as part of the selection at my business.

—Gregory Reeves

In May of 2006, Gregory Reeves opened a retail boutique in the heart of the Greenwich Village neighborhood of New York City – ***christopher19design collective***.

Other Schiffer Books by Ani Afshar:
Beading Necklaces with Ani Afshar
Beads & Strings Jewelry

Library of Congress Control Number: 2007927254

Designed by Mark David Bowyer
Type set in Zurich Blk BT / Korinna BT

ISBN: 978-0-7643-2730-8
Printed in China

Published by Schiffer Publishing Ltd.
4880 Lower Valley Road
Atglen, PA 19310
Phone: (610) 593-1777; Fax: (610) 593-2002
E-mail: Info@schifferbooks.com

In Europe, Schiffer books are distributed by
Bushwood Books
6 Marksbury Ave.
Kew Gardens
Surrey TW9 4JF England
Phone: 44 (0) 20 8392-8585; Fax: 44 (0) 20 8392-9876
E-mail: info@bushwoodbooks.co.uk
Website: www.bushwoodbooks.co.uk
Free postage in the U.K., Europe; air mail at cost.

Contents

5-strand Necklace 4

3-strand Necklace 20

3-strand Pearl Bracelet 31

Ani Afshar's Gallery of Beaded Fantasies 41

5-strand Necklace

For this 5-strand necklace we will use 30-guage oxidized sterling silver wire.

Cut wire 50" long for the 15" finished necklace. Notice the entire palette of bead colors and types shown in this image.

String one bead and fold over at the center. Holding the bead with one hand and the two wire ends with the other hand, roll the bead to twist the two wire ends close to the bead together (about two inches).

Put 5 small beads on one of the silver strands and twist the wires together, leaving space in between.

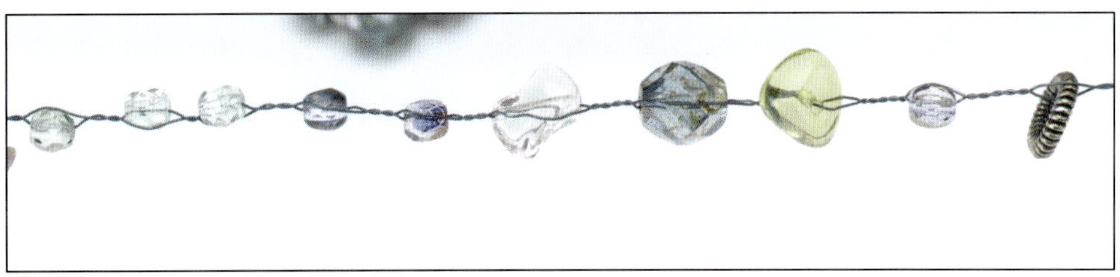

Put more beads of various sizes, color, and shapes on one of the wire strands. Twist the wires together, capturing the beads at various intervals and leaving approximately even spaces between the beads.

String more beads, including one large (purple) bead for the first strand.

Continue beading and twisting the wire.

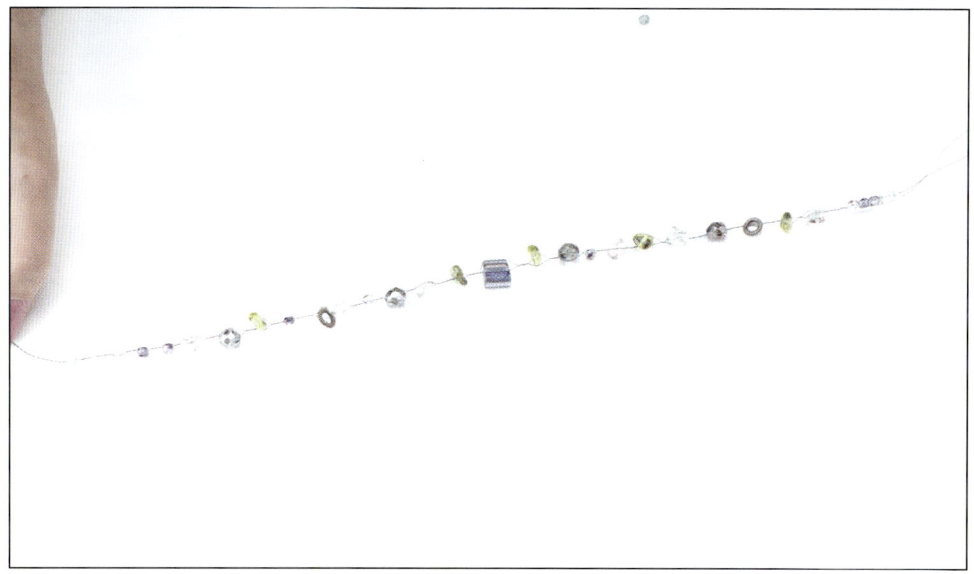

Ending with about 5 small beads.

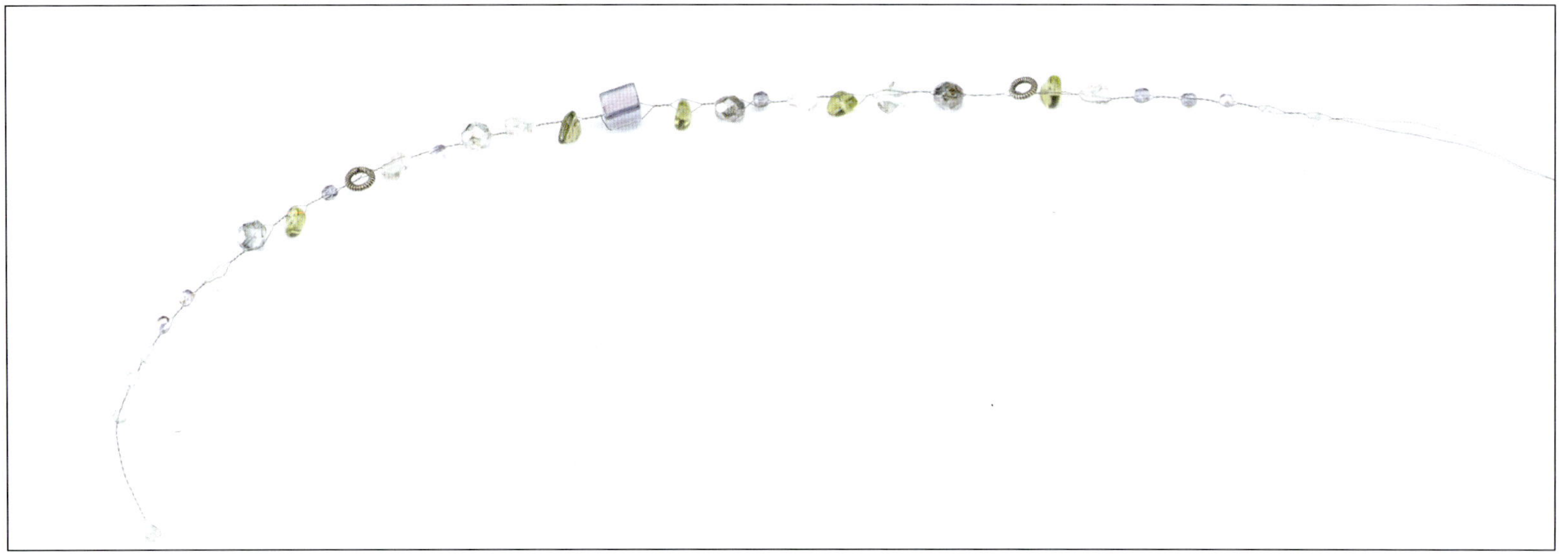

The first strand is complete.

Cut the wire for the second strand. There will be five strands in all for this necklace.

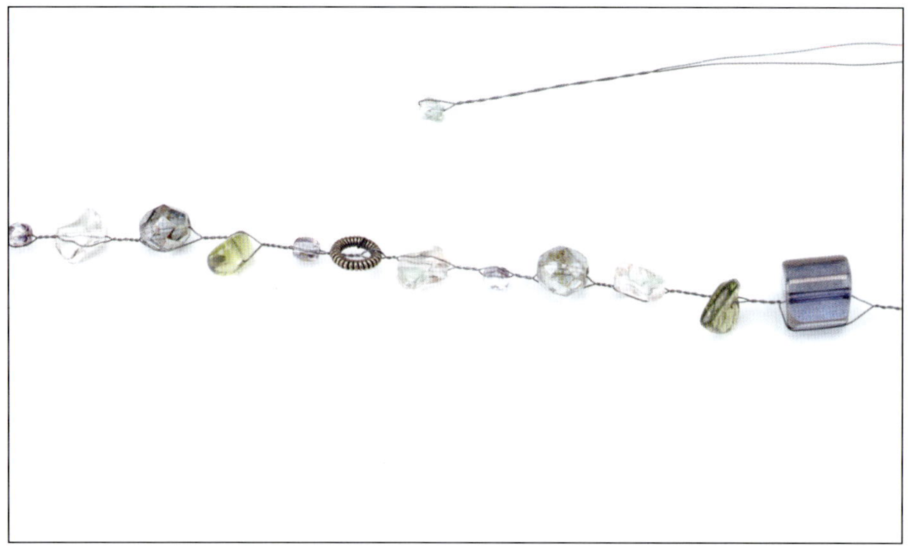

Beginning the second strand, the first bead is in place and the wire is twisted.

The first strand had five small beads at the end. The second strand has six beads at the end. The idea is not to get the same size or color beads side by side on the five strands.

Continue stringing beads and twisting the wire strands, sequencing them in a way that will not put the same beads side-by-side on the 5 strands.

Sometimes it is easier to twist the strands while holding them vertically.

Four strands are beaded and twisted. Use one really big bead per strand.
Repeat for 5 strands, always trying to sequence the beads in a way that won't put them side-by-side and including one large bead per strand.

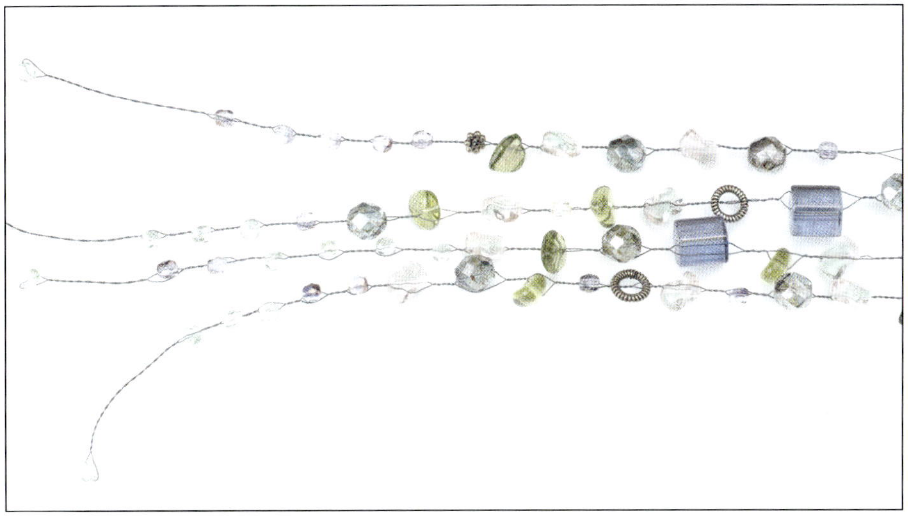

As you continue, check to make sure your separations are even between the strands.

You can get the spacing right before you twist the strands, as shown here.

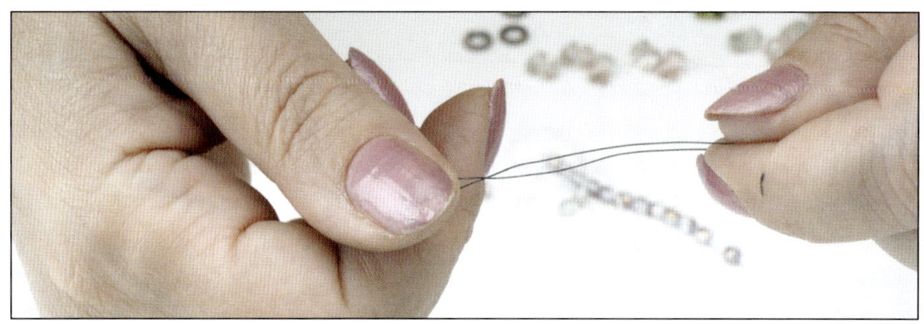

Complete the fifth strand.

All five strands are complete. Notice there is only one large (purple in this case) bead per strand.

Twist the ends of all five strands together to form a single necklace out of the individual strands.

Now it is time to put the clasp on the necklace.

Fold a 5-inch, 24-guage oxidized silver wire in half.

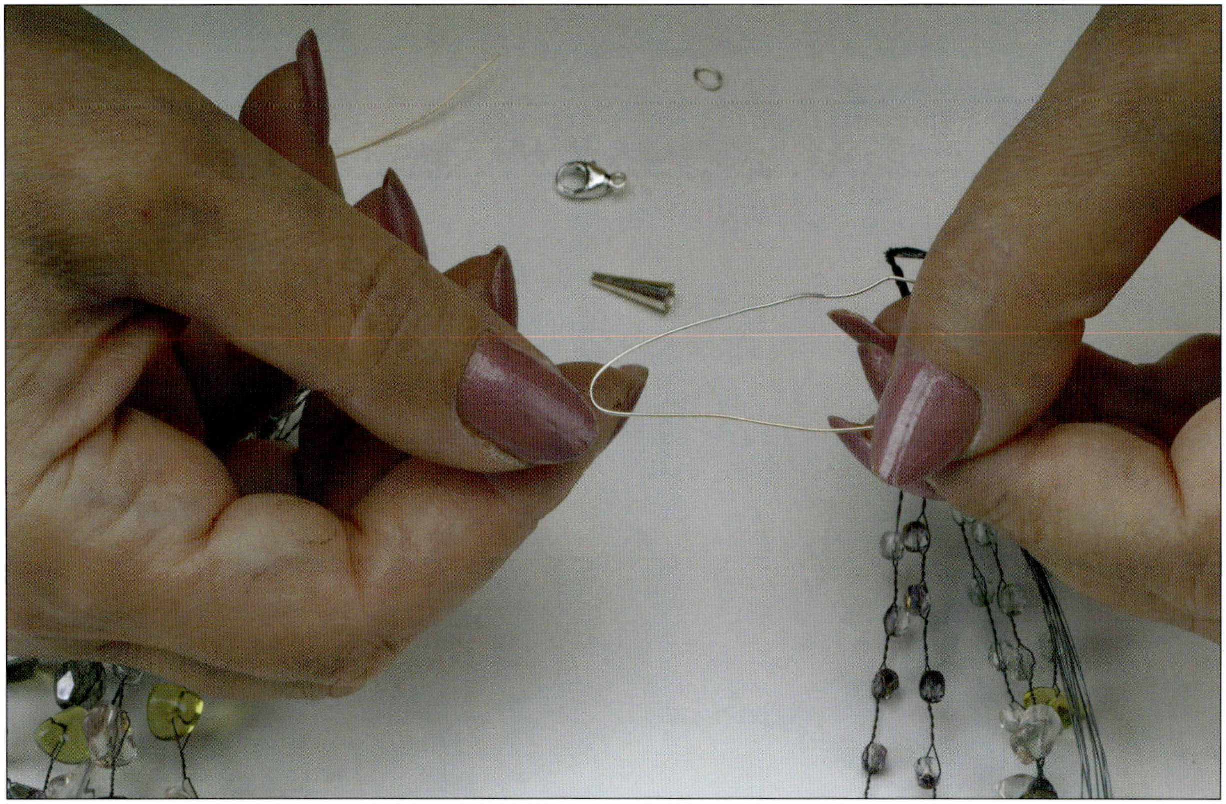

Wrap the loose ends of the necklace around the folded end of this wire.

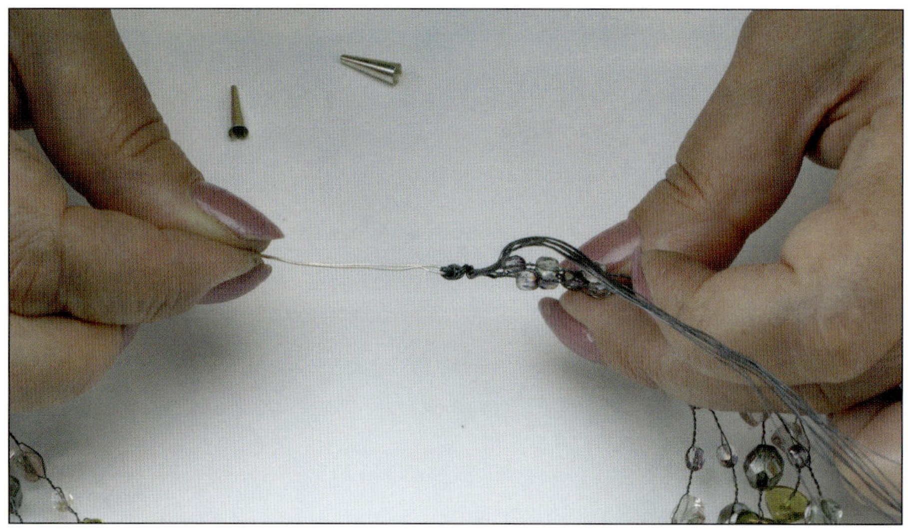

Wrap the loose ends around, twisting them together, as shown.

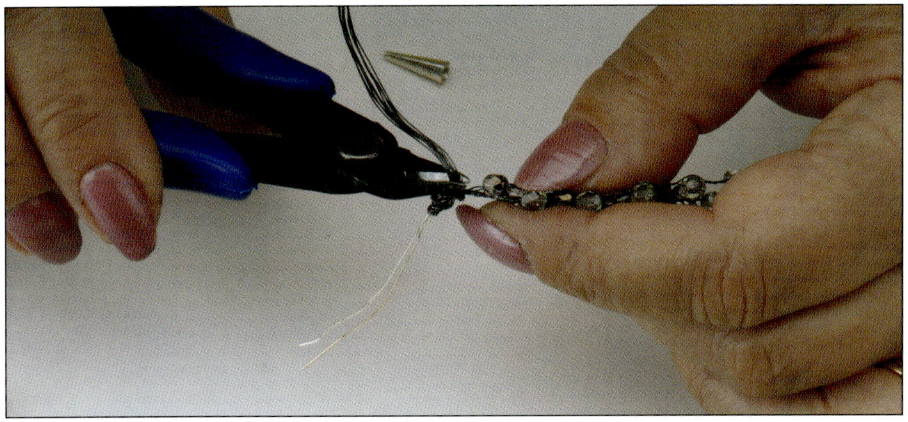

Cut the excess wires on the necklace.

Like so.

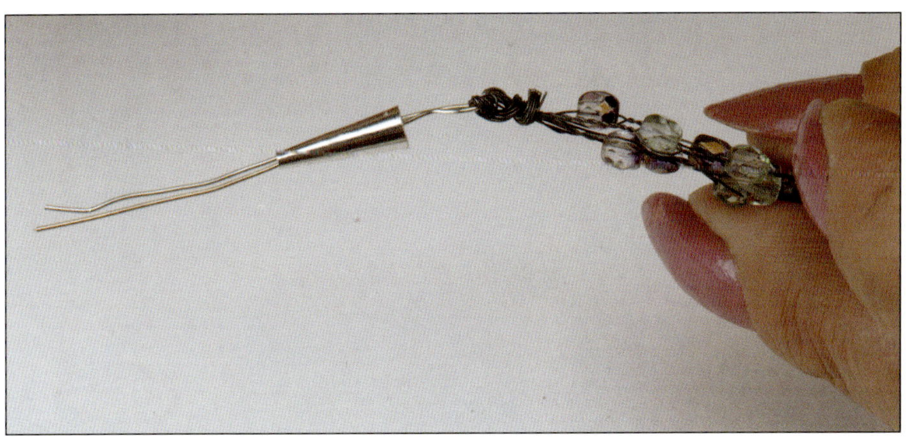

Slide the cone on the two folded wire ends.

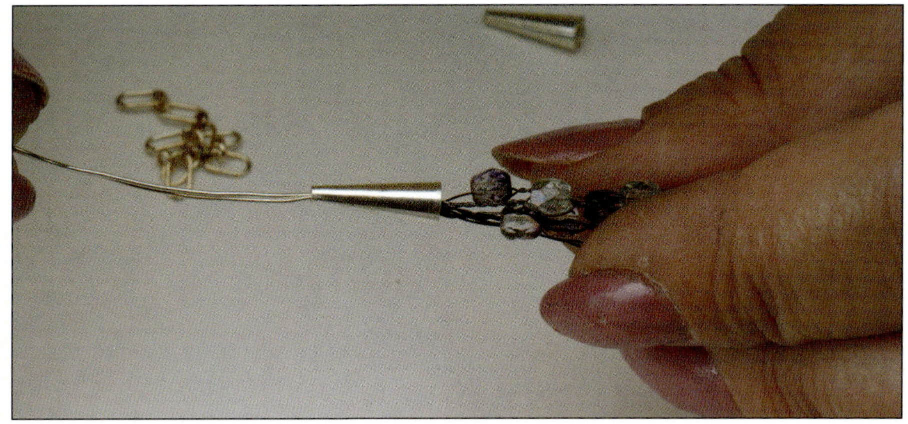

Push the cone down tightly so it covers everything.

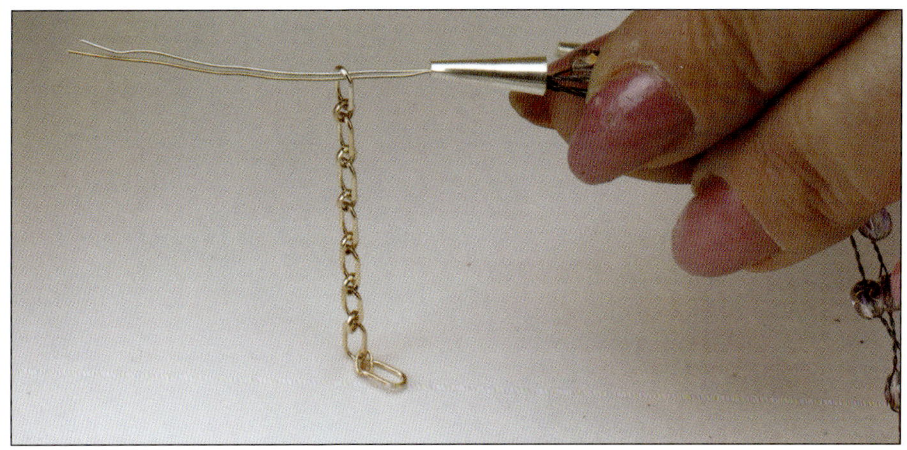

Slide the extension chain on the two wire ends.

Using round-nose pliers, first fold over the two wire ends and then wrap it tightly and evenly around the small end of the cone.

Like so.

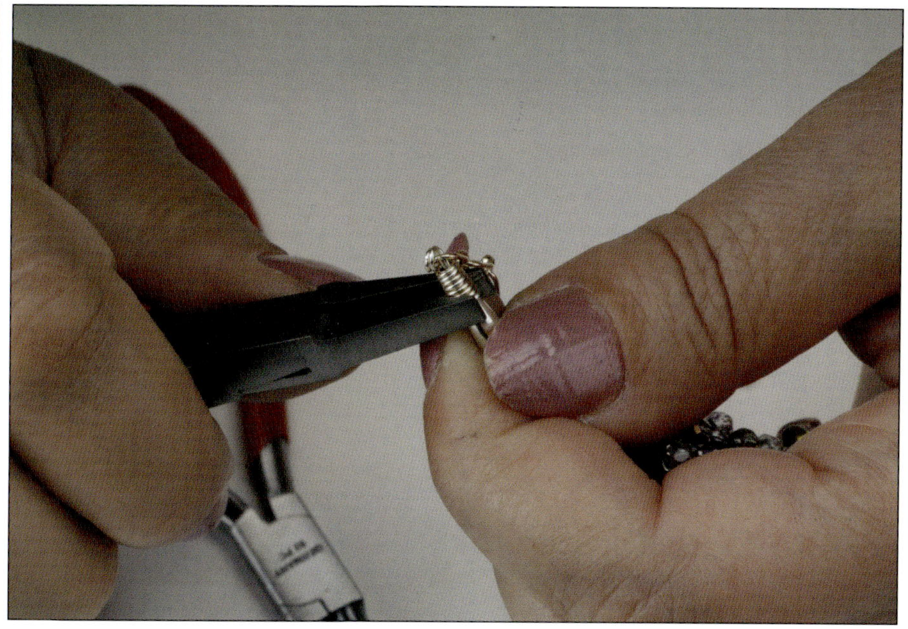

Smoothing the end of the wire.

Cut off the loose end of the wrapped wire and flatten it with the flat-nosed pliers.

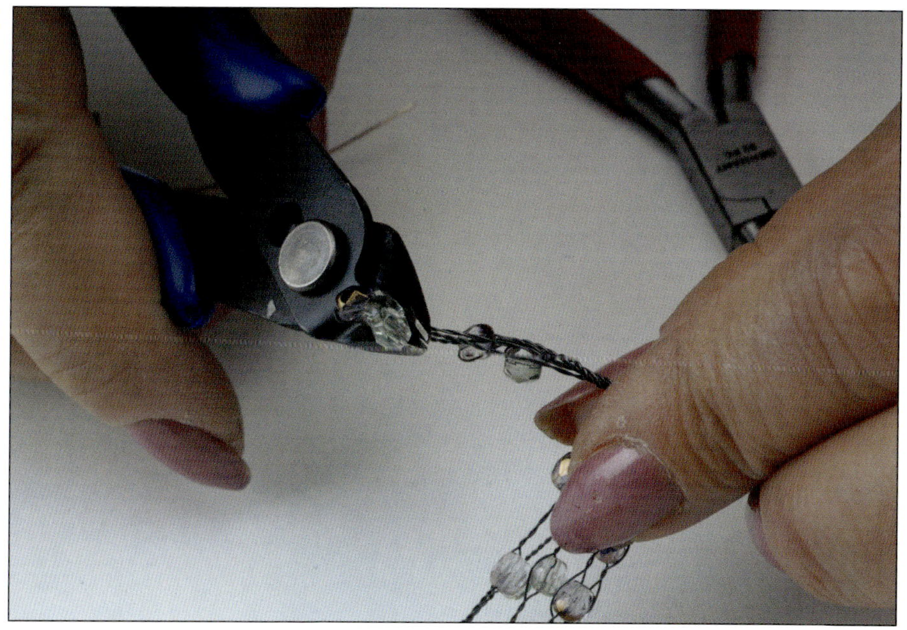

On the other side of the necklace, cut the extra end beads off with cutters.

Place the cone the same way as the other end, but do not put the extension chain on.

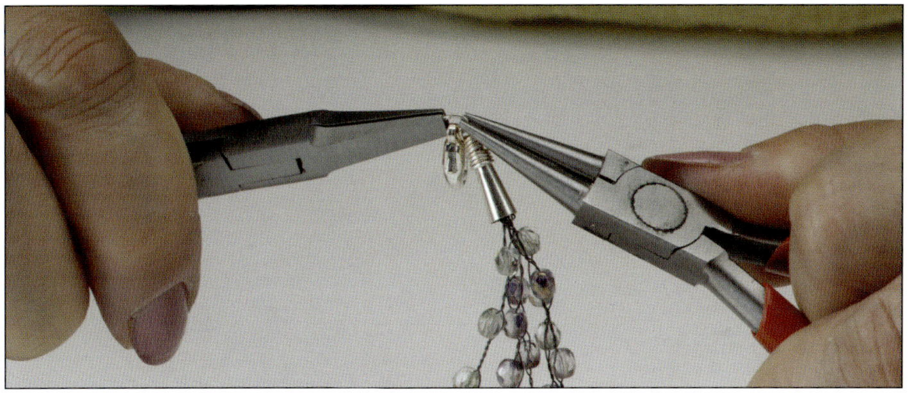

Using a jump ring, connect the clasp to this side.

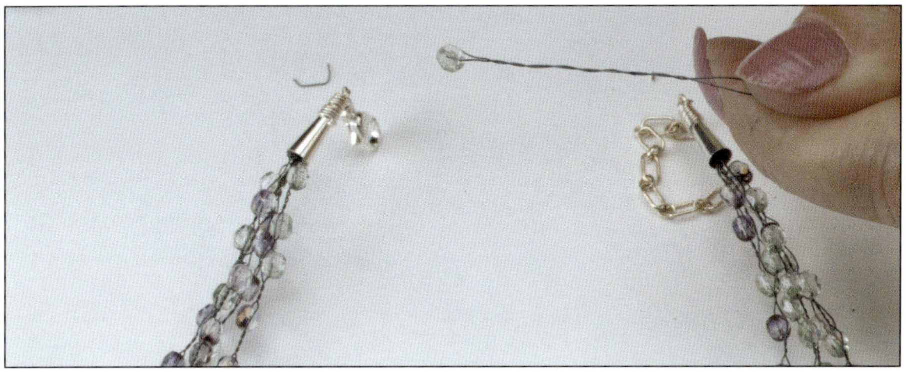

We finish it off with one bead at the end of the extension chain. Slide a bead on a thin wire, fold the wire in half at the center where the bead is located, and twist the wire to secure the bead.

Thread the twisted wire through the end of the chain.

Secure the bead to the end of the chain by looping it with the round-nosed pliers.

This necklace is complete.

3-strand Necklace

For this 3-strand necklace, we will use 28-guage (heavier) vermeil (18 karat gold plated sterling silver) wire because we are using heavier beads.

The color pallet for this necklace includes gray pearls and turquoise nuggets.

The beading process begins the same way as the first necklace.

Stringing one strand and twisting the wires together to capture the beads at intervals, beginning with small beads.

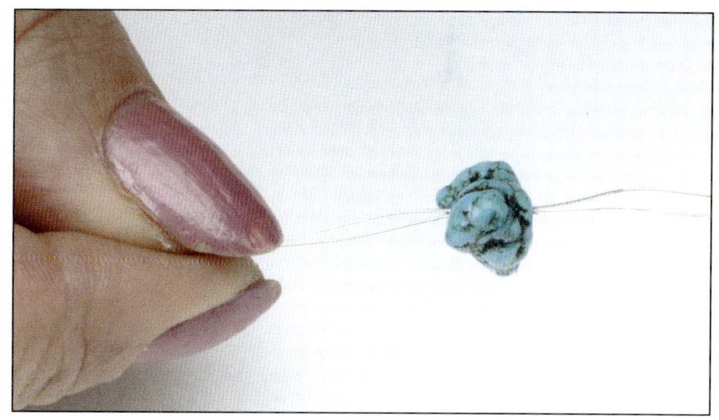

For the large turquoise nugget, put both wires through the hole. Position the nugget in place.

Depending on the size of the hole, run either one or both strands of wire back through the hole.

Like so. Pull the wire tight so the loop closes around the bead. The large bead is now secure.

The smaller beads are twisted into place, just as before, by stringing one wire and twisting the two wires, one at a time.

Repeating the process of stringing a large turquoise nugget.

Like so.

Continue stringing and twisting. Once you've settled on your color and bead choices, there is no set sequence for the beading. Arrange them in an order that pleases you. Only keep in mind that as you create additional strands, the beads should fall into the gaps created in the preceding strands.

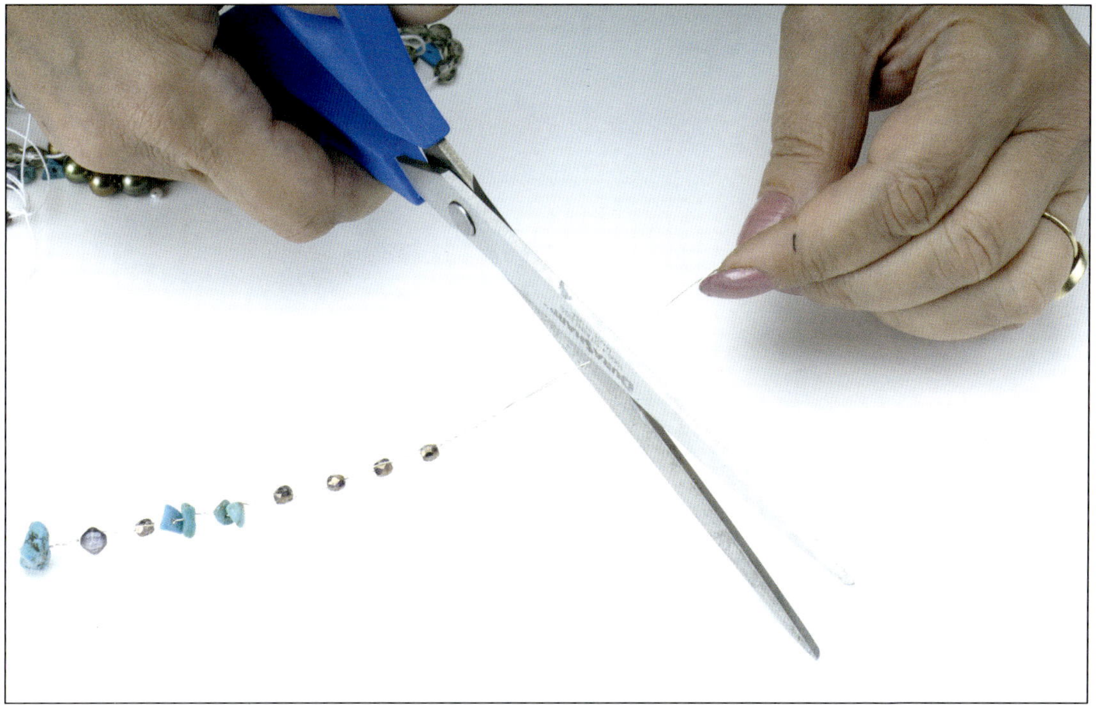

The first strand is complete. Cut the excess loose.

Cutting the second strand of wire. Notice that if you don't have wire cutters, scissors will do the job.

The first bead of the second strand is now twisted into place.

Remember to begin with the small beads at the end. Beads may get larger after that.

Check your spacing as you go. I want this necklace to include more turquoise so I will be repeating turquoise beads here to create an overall effect.

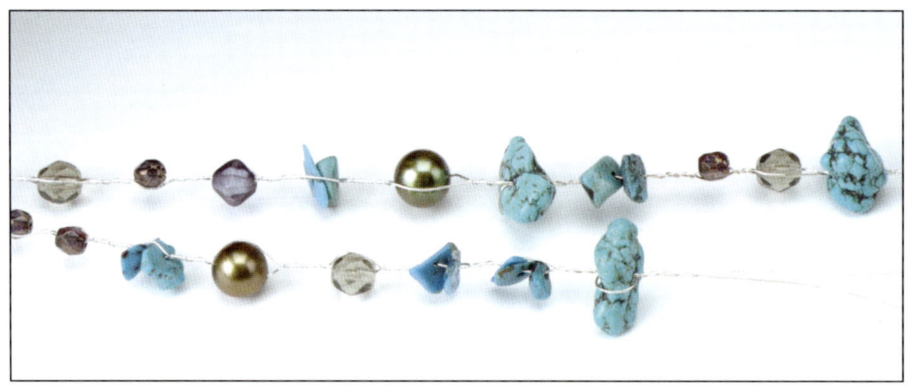

Stringing the large turquoise beads in the same way as before.

Intersperse big and small beads to create a texture, using more turquoise to create a predominantly turquoise necklace.

The first two strands are complete.

Beginning the third strand, keep the separations going. Continue adding beads and twists.

Check regularly to make sure you are getting the beads in the places you want and are creating the look you desire.

The three strands are complete.

Twist all three strands together, as you did before with the first necklace.

The first two projects so far. Nearly complete.

Repeat the steps for finishing the first necklace on the second project, first adding the wire, cone, and extension chain to one side …

… and then adding the wire, cone, and clasp to the other side.

Add the bead to the end of the extension chain …

… and the necklace is complete.

3-strand Pearl Bracelet

We will be using 24-guage (heavier) vermeil wire.

The third project will be a pearl bracelet with three strands. Here's the bead color palette. The wire used here is a thicker 24 gauge gold-plated silver wire.

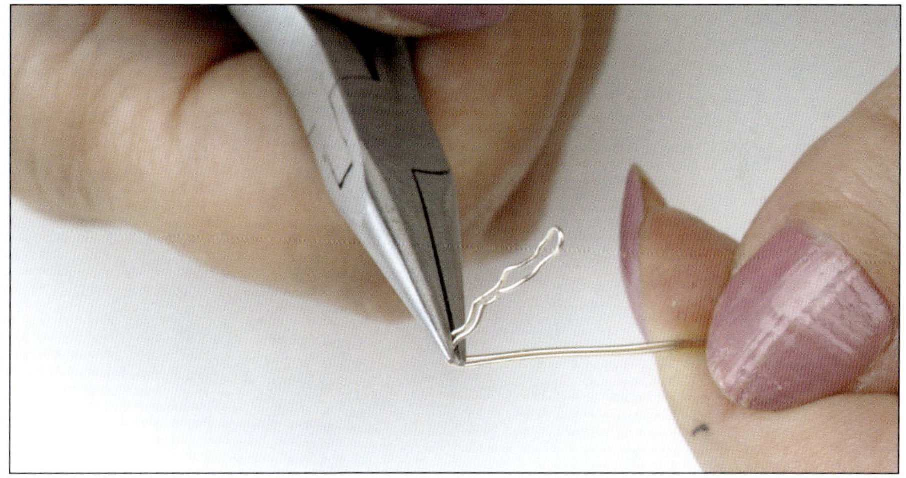

Pinch the wires with the pliers and fold over.

Cut two equal lengths of wire measuring about five times the circumference of your wrist. Using round nosed pliers, we're going to create a loop at one end, holding the two wires together.

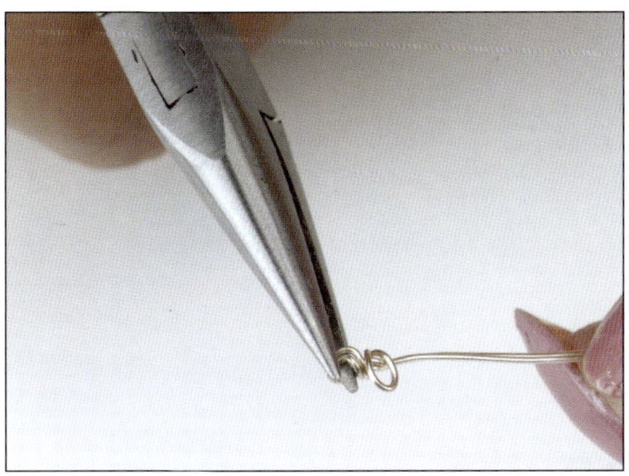

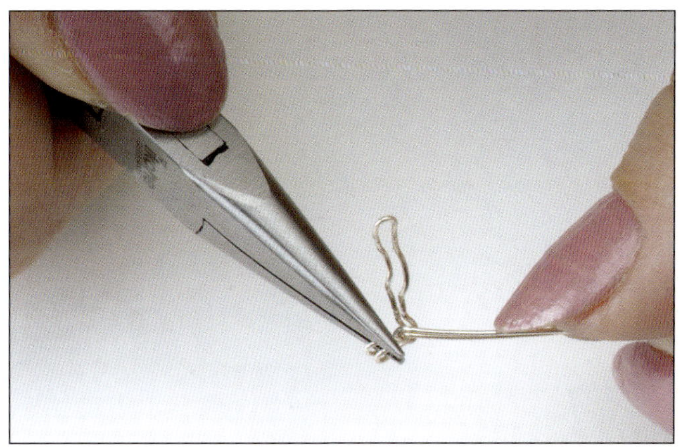

Wrap the folded wires over and around the piers creating a loop.

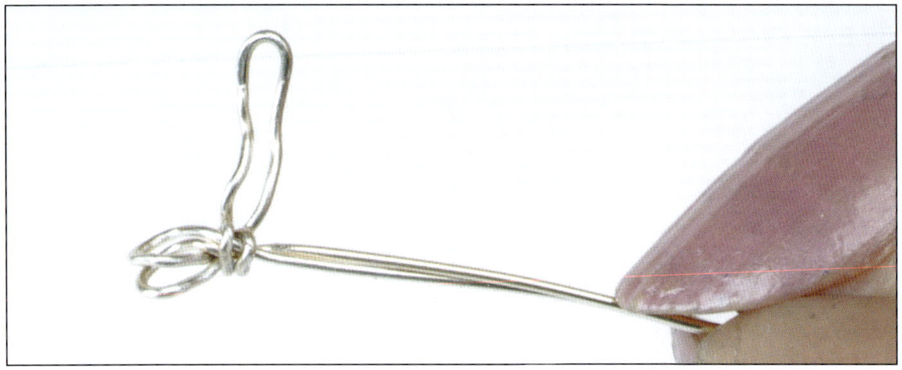

Wrap twice to make sure it holds. Now you have a loop. You'll use cutters to snip off the excess wire at the base of the loop and smooth out with flat-nose pliers.

Start stringing your beads. The first bead should be a small bead and close to the loop. Because this is a bracelet, we are using a heavier, 24-gauge wire.

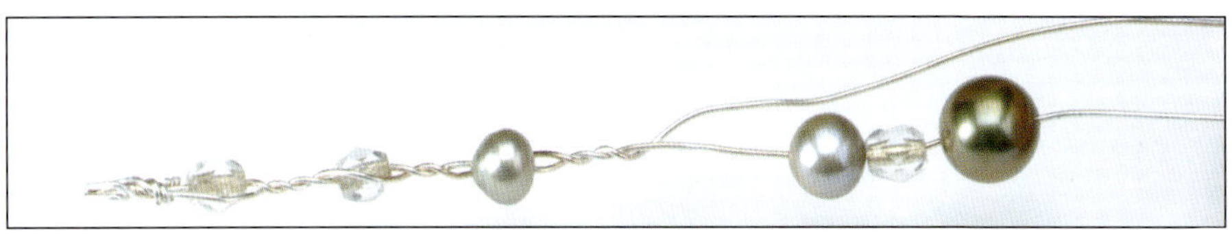

The first few pearls are twisted in place. Use the same twist and spacing as in the necklaces.

The twists are much thicker with the heavier wire.

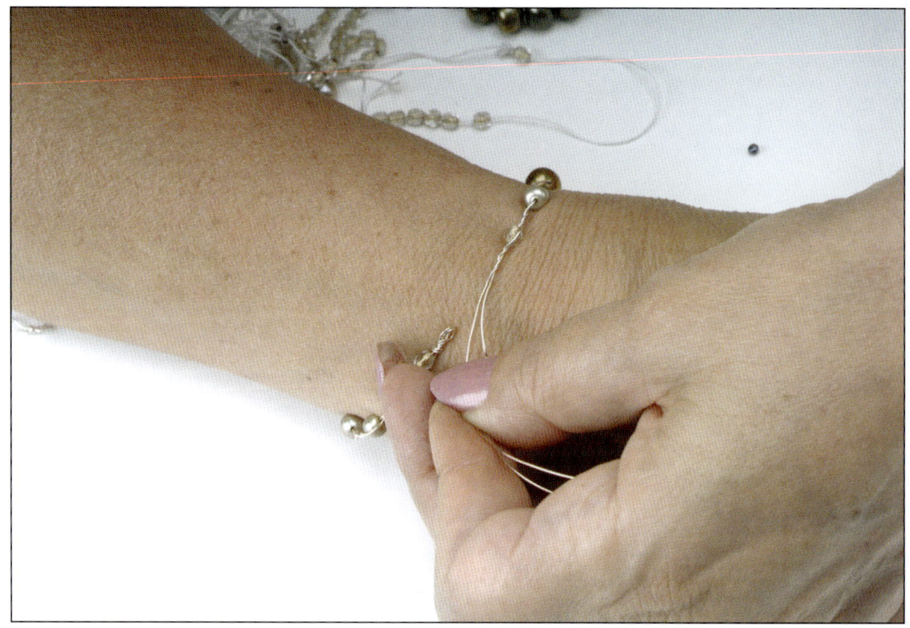

Measure the bracelet around your wrist as you go, to make sure it is long enough when complete, remembering that another inch and a half will be added while assembling.

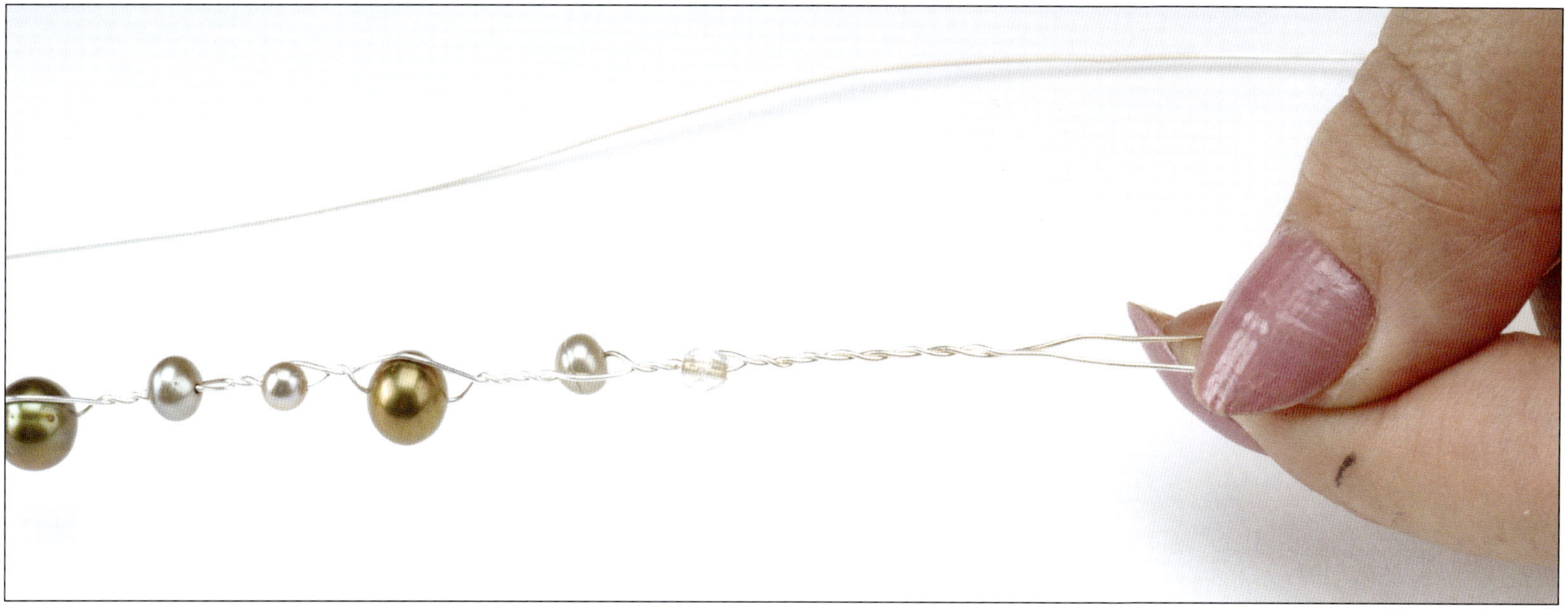

Make a 1-1/2-inch twist without beads. **Do not cut.**

Make a sharp fold in the middle of the 1-1/2-inch twisted wire. Do not cut.

As before, start with a small bead after the fold, at the end of the bracelet. Add pearls and beads and twist.

Our two strands are complete. Notice the larger pearls are in the middle of each strand.

Twist and fold the wire again to begin the third and final strand of this bracelet.

Start stringing the pearls and twisting the wire on the third strand, using the same way as before. Do not cut off strands.

The three strands are complete.

Use your round-nosed pliers to make a loop the same way as at the start and cut off the extra wire.

Twist the folded end of the 3-strand bracelet to create a loop with round-nose pliers.

Repeat with the second fold.

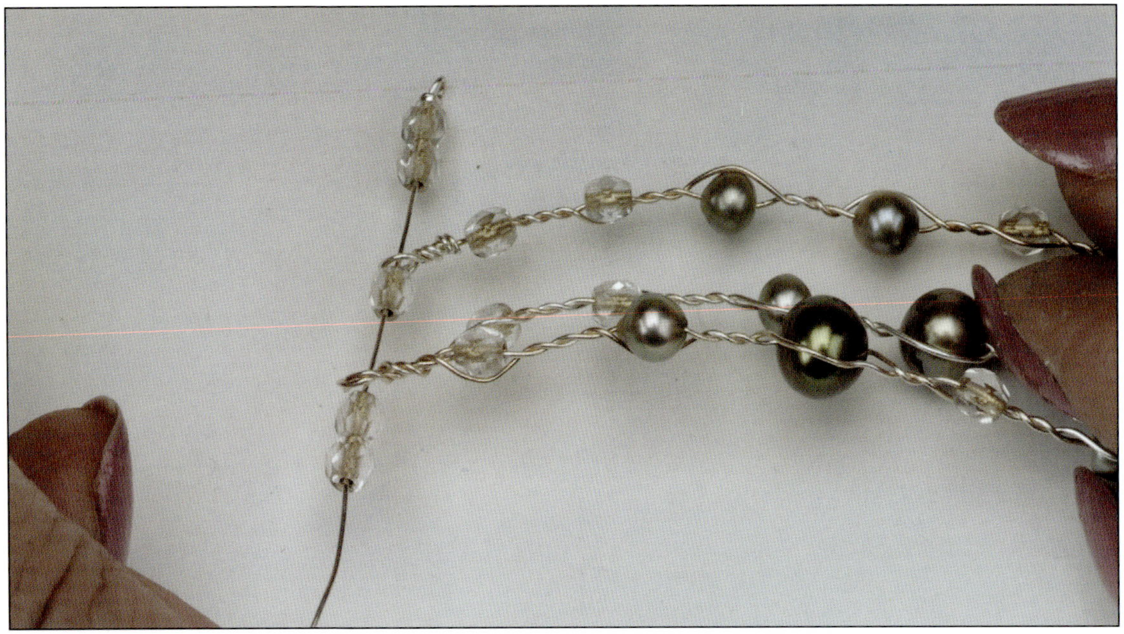

Make a small ring at the end on a 5-inch piece of 24-guage wire. Place two small beads on the 5-inch looped wire. Run this wire through the two loops at one end of the bracelet, with two beads on either side and a single bead in the center between the loops.

Pull them tightly together.

Put the end of the wire through the loop.

Pull it tightly together.

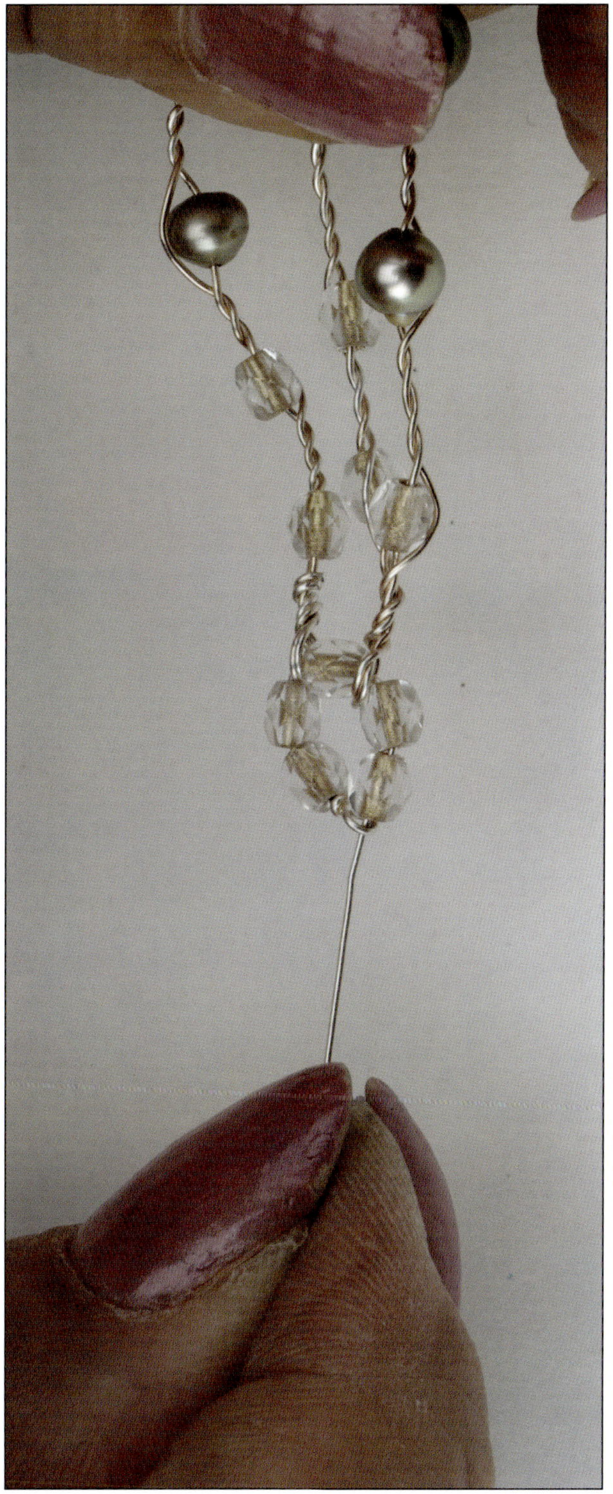

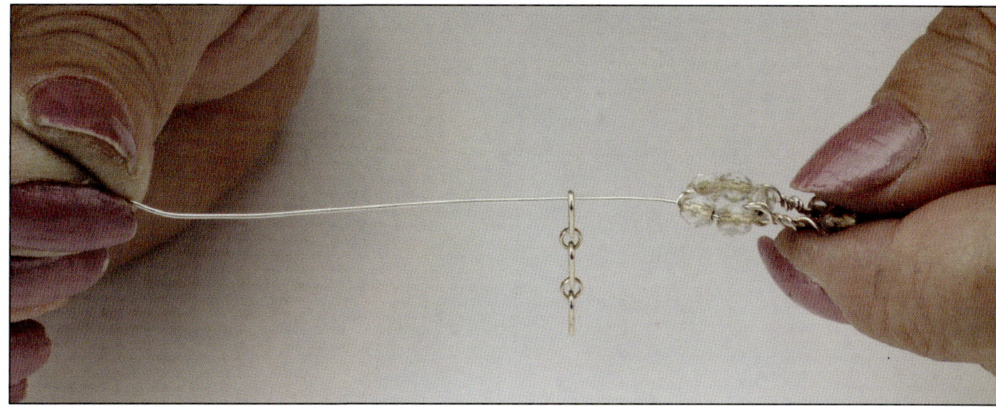

Add a little bit of end chain on the wire.

Make a small loop, securing the end chain in place and making a triangle.

Repeat the process on the other side, but without the end chain.

With a jump ring, connect the clasp to the loop.

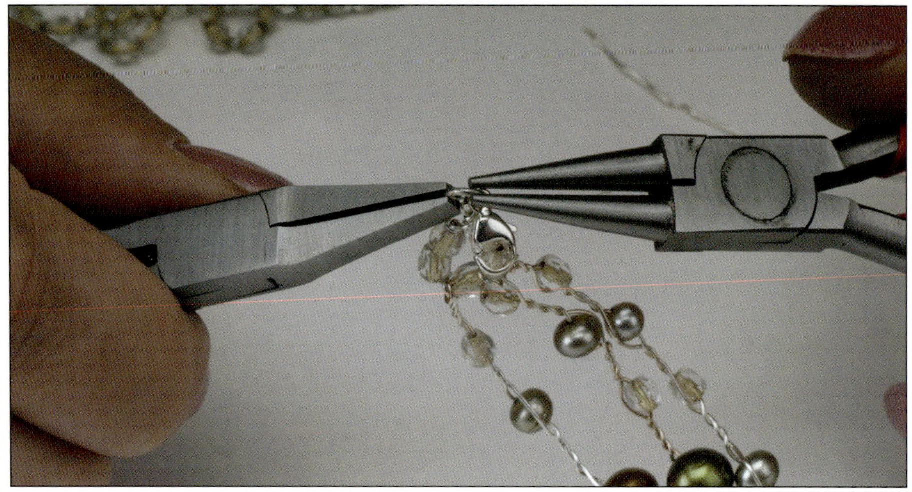

Close the jump fin, and you're done.

The completed bracelet.

Ani Afshar's Gallery of Beaded Fantasies